THE RETURN OF THE SACRED

The Return of the Sacred

BY

JOOST DE BLANK

FOREWORD BY

THE ARCHBISHOP OF CANTERBURY

THE FAITH PRESS
7 Tufton Street, London, S.W.1

MOREHOUSE-BARLOW CO. INC., NEW YORK, U.S.A.

FIRST PUBLISHED IN 1968

© *Joost de Blank*

PRINTED IN GREAT BRITAIN
in 11 point Baskerville type
BY THE FAITH PRESS LTD
LEIGHTON BUZZARD
SBN 7164 0005 7

Dedicated to all, both clergy and laity, with whom I am privileged to work at Westminster Abbey, and who, from the oldest resident in the Precincts to the youngest choirboy, from the Dean to the most junior member of the Clerk of Works' staff, have become my very close friends, and who have, one and all, heartened and encouraged me in the House of my Pilgrimage.

The Little Cloister
Westminster Abbey
February–June, 1967

ACKNOWLEDGMENTS

Acknowledgments are due to the following for the short quotations from—

Malcolm Boyd: *Are You Running With Me, Jesus?*
William Heinemann Ltd.; S.C.M. Press Ltd., London,
1966; and Holt, Rinehart and Winston, New York.

Material from the Jerusalem Bible in © 1966 Darton,
Longman & Todd Ltd. and Doubleday & Co. Inc.,
and is used by permission of the publishers.

CONTENTS

FOREWORD

By the Archbishop of Canterbury

This book will greatly help its readers in their understanding of the Christian calling in the world to-day. The word *sacred* has always meant *belonging to God* or *set apart for God*, and there has at times been a wide gulf in people's minds between things which are sacred and things which are ordinary or common. And a narrow view of what is sacred has often isolated religion from everyday life. In recent times the reaction from this narrow view has caused many people, including religious people, to dismiss the idea of the sacred as outmoded and to try to pursue the good life without it.

The author of this book combines immense experience of human problems, in the East End of London, in South Africa and latterly in England again, with deep thought about the meaning of Christianity. His theme is the re-assertion of the *sacred* and the meaningfulness of the sacred for ordinary human life. The sacred is not a realm apart, but the true meaning of the world itself, because God created the world for fellowship with Himself. All people and all things are designed by God to be sacred, and the disciplined going apart with God to which Christian people are still called is no escapism but a witness to the sacred meaning of all existence.

✝ MICHAEL CANTUAR :

INTRODUCTION

THE swinging pendulum is among the most hackneyed of clichés. But it is hard to find a better. Arnold Toynbee's withdrawal and return is a swinging pendulum; so is our Lord's 'Come unto me' followed by His 'Go ye into all the world'. And so, for that matter is prayer and work: we must not pray so unremittingly that there is no time to do anything else; and we must not lose ourselves so completely in our work that prayer is crowded out.

It is part of the human condition to live in a state of tension—our individual wishes and our family responsibilities, our private interests and our public lives, our earning our livings, and our pursuing our hobbies; the list is endless, and the cut and thrust of the struggle has been the novelists' theme since fiction began to be written.

In the current attitude of Christians to their Faith, the tension is very evident between the secular and the sacred. Some would see this tension epitomized in the difference between two such newspapers as *The New Christian* and *The Church Times*. In a belief that the pendulum had swung much too far in the Church's emphasis on the sacred, so much so that it was almost out of touch with everyday life, the 'secular' Christians gave the pendulum a sharp push in the other direction. As a result there are many to-day who believe that the secularization of the Church has gone too far. One of the keenest and best-known exponents of this point of view is Mr. Malcolm Muggeridge, that more than interesting monk *manqué*, who may yet end up within the walls of a cloister. But do we want his kind of Church, which in effect calls for the abdication of all social responsibility, and concentrates its activities solely on the spiritual cultivation of the individual?

In such an attitude Mr. Muggeridge and Dr. Goebbels

are strange bed-fellows, but this is the line which the Nazis took. They would have no quarrel, they said, with the Church while it continued its proper work of preparing men's souls for the life to come, but the moment it dared to speak to the State or the human situation generally, it was exceeding its authority and was thus jeopardizing its own future, as well as its true purpose.

This book is written with no intention of supporting such a creed, for it is a denial of the basic fact of Christianity that distinguishes it from all other religions. The central truth of the Christian Faith lies in the belief that God became man in Jesus Christ, and that 'the Word was made flesh and dwelt among us'. God has therefore set His seal on the whole of life. Nothing lies outside His concern, and there is as grave danger in trying to separate the social from the individual, as there is in trying to isolate the sacred from the secular.

Jesus, at the beginning of His public life, came preaching that the Kingdom of Heaven was at hand. Now whatever else the Kingdom means it is certainly not limited to a person's private spiritual development. It must include man's life in society, with all that this means in terms of race, nation, politics, economic well-being and educational opportunity.

When a pendulum describes too big an arc in either direction, the chances are that it will get itself caught up in some way—and the clock will stop. Sometimes, like Rip van Winkle, it may fail to note the passage of time for as much as twenty years, when it is roughly or tenderly released, and the clock starts going again.

If the Church for a number of years was snared by an over-concern for the sacred, with a consequential irrelevance to the world, has it now been trapped by a desire to lose itself in the ordinary life of mankind with no sense of the sacred at all? Its need to immerse itself more and more deeply in the secular world is beyond question. Our Lord's Incarnation peremptorily demands it. And here the Athanasian Creed can come to our help. Perhaps it is not quite so out of date as we sometimes like to think. Of Christ it says:

> For the right faith is, that we believe and confess that our Lord Jesus Christ, the Son of God, is God and man; God, of the substance of the Father, begotten before the worlds; and man, of the substance of his Mother, born in the world.
> Perfect God, and perfect man, of a reasonable soul and human flesh subsisting;
> Equal to the Father as touching his Godhead; and inferior to the Father, as touching his manhood;
> Who, although he be God and man, yet he is not two, but one Christ;
> One: not by the conversion of the Godhead into flesh; but by taking of the manhood into God;
> One altogether; not by confusion of substance, but by unity of person;
> For as the reasonable soul and flesh is one man; so God and man is one Christ.

Our Lord is reported as saying: 'As the Father hath sent me, even so send I you'; and the apostle reminds us: 'As he is, so are we in this world'. Hence there is an identification of Christ with His Church that may not be ignored. And the mission of the Church, both Head and Body, is one: not the conversion of the Godhead into flesh, but the taking of the manhood into God.

In this period of mental and social upheaval, the Church needs desperately to keep calm, with its many tensions (some of which have a psychological rather than a spiritual origin) resolved in a freely swinging pendulum. The Church must always be ready to acknowledge the truth from whatever source it comes. Because it is as diverse as humanity itself, it will exhibit humanity's many-sided facets—the activism of the West, but also the meditation of the East; the requirements of society, but also the needs of the individual; the historical revelation of the Scriptures, but also the existential approach of modern man.

As Professor Keet, the great Afrikaner theologian once wrote: 'There is only one form of apartheid known to Scripture; and that is separation from sin'. Very seldom, except for sin, does the Church have to take up an 'either . . . or' attitude. Rather is it, as the B.B.C. reminded us a few years ago, 'Not only . . . but also'.

Should the pendulum swing too high in one direction and be held fast as a result, great responsibility rests on those who seek to release it, that they do it as tenderly as possible, and not brusquely or roughly—above all not arrogantly.

This then is the object of this book. It is written in the conviction that there is a proper rhythm in the expression of Christianity both in the Church and in the individual disciple. The author has neither the right nor the desire to set himself over against the arguments of the Christian secularists or those who, for want of a better term, might be called Christian pietists. He recognizes, thankfully, the contribution which both schools of thought have brought to to-day's continuing witness. He is grateful to both, but, if his interest must be declared, he believes that secularization may go too far if the sacred nature and practice of our Faith are disregarded. To stress the sacred without rejecting the secular is this book's purpose. The writer may not have been successful, but he has no doubt that the effort ought to be made.

I. THE SACRED REALITY

MAN is by nature a worshipping animal. This, so far as he can perceive, is what distinguishes him from other living creatures and gives him a status all his own. He may sometimes feel that he has grown out of all the religious mumbo-jumbo in which he was brought up; but take away from him the opportunity of worshipping his maker, and he will fabricate gods of his own design and to his own desires. For worship he must. These other gods in the twentieth century are generally not the graven images against which he is solemnly warned in the Ten Commandments, but they are gods none the less. False gods which provide an outlet for man's deepest longings, and relief from his profoundest fears.

If a man worships money or power or sexual or intellectual prowess, this is not usually recognized as a religious activity. But why not? The god he has chosen to serve calls for wholehearted sacrifice and allegiance. These are characteristic of all true worship, though the practice often goes unrecognized when the object of man's homage is thought to be merely mundane or temporal.

When that happens, as often as not people look for the sacred in some of life's irrational or inexplicable happenings. For example, they grow superstitious. For nine-tenths of their lives they pride themselves on being hard-headed and down to earth men and women, but with the remaining one-tenth, they could not be more gullible. They read in the papers what the stars foretell; they go and have their fortunes told; they will not go on a journey without taking their mascot with them; they will not walk under a ladder, and if the thirteenth day of the month happens to fall on a Friday, they come out in goose pimples just at the thought of it. Of course, a habit of touching wood (or 'knocking on wood' as the phrase has it on the other side of the Atlantic) may be incredibly stupid, like becoming optimistic or hopeful when a black cat crosses one's path. But it is even more stupid to condemn all these practices out of hand. The thing itself may well be silly, but it looks, for all modern man's confident self-sufficiency, as if the supernatural insists on breaking through.

There are very few irreligious people who do not have a superstitious quirk of some kind. It is not to be expected in those who are avowedly religious. Only when religious convictions are discarded, does some irrational fancy have to be found to take their place.

The sense of the sacred cannot easily be expelled, even if we want to rid ourselves of it. It was in 1917 that Rudolf Otto wrote his most famous book *Das Heilige*, translated six years later into English with the title *The Idea of the Holy*. Within half a century this has become a religious classic, demanding to be read by every intelligent student of theology, layman or cleric. For all its popularity its arguments go largely unheeded. With the ever wider adoption of the so-called scientific method in all forms of education, everything which cannot be explained in scientific terms has to be ruled out.

We shall be making a great mistake if we think that the world as a whole is becoming increasingly secular, if by secular we mean exclusively what man can understand and control for himself. Half of the world has become Communist, but it would be incredibly naïve to assume that all Communists are self-conscious Marxists who have studied and made their own the master's materialistic philosophy. Marx as a Jew retained, albeit unwittingly, an apocalyptic view of history. It does not have to be called a 'day of the Lord', but the irruption into history of the unhistorical moment when the State will vanish away has all the signs of apocalypse as Jews and Christians have understood it. It is an irrational event, that is, an event which because it is entirely unknown remains a vision which has no present counterpart in reality. It is, in fact, an invasion of the secular by the sacred.

Furthermore, there is no doubt that millions of those who live in the Communist part of the world are fanatical in their allegiance. The Red Guards who venerate the words of Chairman Mao Tse Tung as being verbally inspired, and in some form or other a panacea for all their ills, are exactly similar to those who regard the Bible as having been given word by word by God to His people, and who brush off criticism by asserting that the words have meaning only for the elect, the chosen people. In other words the Communist Revolution calls for an act of faith beyond reason, and its theorems and principles are not subject to rational scrutiny but have to be vindicated in action. Its devotees exhibit a mystical reverence for Marx and for Lenin, who are respectively the Yahweh and Moses of Communism.

In little more than twenty years since the war, we have seen the member-states of the United Nations grow from 30 to 120. This rapid growth has been almost entirely due to the achieving of independent status by formerly dependent countries. Those men and women who risked death and suffered exile and imprisonment to secure national independence are for the most part worthy of honour and respect. But it would be stupid to believe that such beliefs as UHURU (Freedom) or Independence were not more than manifestations of a developing secular society. For countless nationals, these words took on a millennial aura—so much so that when independence was eventually granted, many were bitterly disillusioned when the great day did not bring in the Kingdom of God with a bang!

It is true that they would not have defined their disillusionment thus. They would assert that theirs was a political movement, but it was clearly far more than this, far more than merely a secular evolution or revolution.

All over the world there has been a retreat of the sacred before the encroachments of the secular. But only a little thought is needed to show that when the secular has won some bridge-head, its well-entrenched positions elsewhere are hurled back into the sea.

In addition to these indisputable happenings not yet fully explained, indeed with scientific research scarcely begun, there is also the fact of sin, which Charles Davis in his valuable little book, *God's Grace in History*,[1] defines as the inexplicable invasion of the irrational in an otherwise rational being. Why is it that again and again respectable man has in honesty to make St. Paul's words his own : 'The good that I would, that I do not; and the evil that I would not, that I do'? When man finds that part of his nature militates against his own best interests, he realizes that in scientific terms he is faced with a problem for which he can offer no solution.

There is another modern piece of evidence which has to be taken into account. Just as intelligent man begins to believe that pretty well the whole of life can be explained in reasonable terms and begins to insist that the Church has no chance of survival unless it gives up its pre-scientific mythologies, at this moment, as if to cock a snook at man's pride and self-sufficiency, we are faced with the incredibly rapid rise of the Pentecostal churches, with their emphasis on the outpouring of the Spirit, generally in tongues unknown and incomprehensible, which are a flat and open negation of the cool and calculating use of reason. These

[1] Collins' Fontana, 5/-.

are gaining hundreds of new adherents at a time when the more traditional Churches are struggling, not altogether successfully, to maintain their position.

There is no doubt that science has evacuated life of many of its former sacred elements. Where before men explained a large number of natural occurrences in terms of God's activity, science now offers a technical solution (though none to account for the uniformity of nature—which science in its own world has to take for granted). This increasing 'desacrilization' of life, as Harvey Cox calls it in his famous book *The Secular City*,[2] is to be welcomed. Man must not foist on to a convenient but unreliable deity what he himself should be quite able to cope with; and the more he can fulfil God's promise to him in the Garden of Eden story to act as lord of creation the better. According to Cox God intervenes, or is seen to intervene, only where men cannot act for themselves. But, he asserts, it is one of the marks of maturity in the human race that man will find this recourse to help outside himself no longer necessary.

There is a fallacy in this argument. It reduces mankind to the stereotype of scientific man, and this is obviously far from true. He may be to-day's popular hero, but he does not express the whole of human personality. Besides him, there is poetic man, musical man, artistic man, organization man and many others.

The intuitions of the poet are an acknowledged form of knowledge, and he is not to be despised. All are acquainted with Wordsworth's ode: 'Intimations of Immortality'. But though in the reader, familiarity may breed indifference if not contempt, this does not deny what the poet has to say. How well we know the words:

2 S.C.M. Press, 21/-.

> Not in entire forgetfulness,
> And not in utter nakedness,
> But trailing clouds of glory, do we come
> From God who is our home :
> Heaven lies about us in our infancy.
>
> At length the Man perceives it die away,
> and fade into the light of common day.

Is this just a poetic conceit or, for all our pedestrianism, have we not all had similar experiences of one sort or another?

Most of us can remember moments when we could see through the opaque veil of our physical condition and human environment, and behold for ourselves 'the light that never was on sea or land'. To us, such incidents appear to be not quite respectable. They do not fit in with modern scientific education, and so we feel better if we hide them or disregard them. But we can be thankful that in these days, when most men are called to be technicians, there is another side to our natures and that from time to time these other elements demand expression. The crime against human beings is not that many of them have to live as hidden poets or artists, but that they should be treated as if they are technicians and nothing more.

One who was in danger of losing his real life was William Blake. He might have been no more than a rebel in politics, had not the driving force of his poetic and artistic imagination made him keep true to his own standards and ideals, however much they were disregarded and mocked at in his day. Now he has become fashionable, which is perhaps not surprising in a time of general conformity. Blake's emphatic non-conformity—though not in the religious sense—has a great appeal. Here are some words of his which indicate the reality of the sacred, in contrast to a merely scientific temper: ' "What", it will be Question'd, "when the Sun rises, do you not see a round disk of fire somewhat like a Guinea?" O no, no, I see an innumerable company of the Heavenly host crying, "Holy, Holy, Holy is the Lord God Almighty".'

It is just as well we are not all William Blakes. The world would be a very uncomfortable place if we were, but we need something of his spiritual imagination and vision. Life is the poorer for his absence from our technological age.

The conviction that the whole of life cannot be assessed by everything we can see and handle is not limited to a handful of poets and literary men. Certainly Beethoven had a strong conviction of the dimension of eternity as he worked to compose his greatest symphonies, his music for the Passion story, and his *Missa Solemnis*.

Gainsborough, the painter, was equally convinced. He made his own position as clear and translucent as some of his matchless landscapes, when he wrote: 'Everything seems full of blossom of some kind, and at every step I take, and on whatever object I turn my eyes, that sublime expression of the Scriptures: "I am the Resurrection and the Life", seems as if uttered near me'. It may be argued that not many artists to-day would take the same attitude to their profession, but it may also be asked whether art itself has been enriched by reason of the change.

There is, I have suggested, a valid way of looking at life which is different from the scientific. But not all scientists live their whole lives in bondage to the scientific method.

Though I have to write in generalizations, I do not wish to imply that all men of science are alike. This is manifestly not so in a variety of ways, including religion and a sense of the sacred. It is interesting to read a book

like Lansing Lamont's *Day of Trinity*,[3] which is concerne
with the development of the atomic bomb, the first experi
mental explosion in Los Alamos in New Mexico and it
first use as a weapon of mass destruction over Hiroshima
Not the least intriguing parts of the book are those dealin;
with the reactions of the many scientists engaged on th
project. Some regarded it as a bit of work and nothin;
more. Others were frightened by its potential for destruc
tion. And a further group stood in awe before the dawnin;
of the nuclear age, which would bring about change
which they were convinced were too vast for man himsel
to handle. To them, this dawn was a sacred moment, witl
which scientific know-how, however able, was incompeten
to deal. And there is clearly a tremendous difference be
tween an Isaac Newton who said that his task as ;
scientist was to 'think God's thoughts after him', and ;
wholly secular scientist who has no use for this kind o1
so-called clap-trap, but believes that all technologica
ability lies within his own grasp.

The representatives of this latter school make certain tha
science deals only with those problems which it can manage
It deliberately leaves all others alone, because it fears tc
expose its ignorance and therefore lose its status as a sacred
cow! The final blow which ends a life of individual
research is the fact of death. To death all men come. And
how incredibly little investigation has been made of the
fact of death and what happens afterwards. It is surely
ridiculous to spend millions upon millions of pounds to send
an astronaut to the moon, and to spend infinitesimally little
on the universal reality of death and its significance.

Naturally any serious examination of death and after
must include the wide field of psychical research. This
cannot be dismissed as just a collection of frauds or of old

[3] Athenaeum, New York, 1965.

ives' tales. Do ghosts really manifest themselves? Are the innumerable examples of communication with loved ones the other side of the grave nothing more than self-deception? What of clairvoyance, telepathy and extra-sensory perception generally? These too retain their mystery. But subjects such as these have on the whole been ignored by the scientific world.

If pressed, men of science may say that these things lie outside their terms of reference, like the fact of beauty or the reality of the artistic imagination. But as death is the one event which no man can escape, and which writes *finis* to the writings of the most brilliant poet or the researches of the most accomplished physicist, it is high time that it was taken seriously by the scientist.

Let me make it clear that I am writing about the fact of death, not the process of dying. This process is of more than lively concern; and everything possible is being done to delay it as much as possible. Indeed, medical knowledge now makes it possible to keep an organism alive long after the mind and, perhaps, the spirit have gone. The life that flickers on is scarcely distinguishable from that of a vegetable. On some strange grounds of the unknown and the unknowable, science is prepared to pursue man to the gate of death, even to delay his passing through it. But the moment he does pass through, science draws the sheet up over his face and leaves him with, humanly speaking, all the questions about death and existence beyond the grave unanswered.

What is true about death is also true about man's little death which he experiences daily when he goes to sleep. In ancient days, the religious professionals were very interested in a man's dreams. Prophets, soothsayers and witch doctors have always regarded them as important. The psychiatrist still does, but he is regarded as living in the twilight periphery of the scientific world, and for all the painstaking efforts of men like Freud and Jung, far too little work has been done on sleep, its nature and its contents.

In the armed services it is easy to think that those items which do not appear in the curriculum or in regimental orders are unimportant. The same is true of natural sciences. Man has a profound awe and respect for the chemist or the physicist, and he is in danger of thinking that those matters with which science does not concern itself must be unimportant. The truth is that science deals with the things it can manage. Just occasionally there may be a break through into a new field, and in consequence a new area of life is captured for the scientific method. But, like all of us, science does not like to reveal its ignorance. And so it erects a thick wall round those things which are beyond its competence—things like death, sleep, extra-sensory perception and psychical research. By refusing to discuss them, science neither admits its lack of knowledge nor does it deny their reality.

In the few paragraphs above, I realize that I can be accused of using words such as science, the scientist and the scientific method too loosely. It is of course true that many men of science are also men of religion, who refuse to regard their researches as being earthed in a material universe. Perhaps I ought to have written with greater accuracy, though with less likelihood of being understood, of the *secular* method and the *secularist*. Secularism is without doubt the most general attitude among thinking people in the West to-day. They believe that a natural explanation can be found for every occurrence on the earth and in the universe generally, and that what little is left of the sacred will be expunged as man's knowledge increases.

Such a contention is unsound. When 'science' has done all that it is able to do, man will still be left with an inexplicable sense of the numinous. The musician has it, the artist has it, and the poet has it. And so, in fact, has the scientist. In the areas of research several have left on record that as they approached the solution of the problem they were studying, it was as if the answer was 'given' to them— it was more than a straightforward outcome of their investigations.

Every perceptive man and woman knows the 'givenness' of certain moments in their lives. They cannot be explained away. And they bear witness to a Sacred Reality in life, which humanity ignores or rejects at its peril.

Our trouble is that this world is so much with us that we are in danger of allowing the sacred to be crowded out altogether. Again and again, modern life is likened to a rat race, which demands all our attention and all our energies just to remain where we are.

W. H. Davies' lines are almost too well known:

> A poor world this, if full of care
> We have no time to stand and stare.

The need is to find time to 'stand and stare'. A man can be so engrossed in the activities of this life that he leaves himself no time to think of anything else. The busy housewife looking after her home and the children is in the same case. Life, secular life, with all its demands—social as well as working—leaves no time for quiet, for stillness of soul, for a dawning recognition that this life does not tell the whole human story.

This is not to decry our secular age; this is not to blame people for their lack of apprehension. We live in a world where the sacred is more and more excluded. Sometimes rightly, as when modern knowledge takes over an area of life which used to be God's. Sometimes not so rightly, as when man allows no time to exercise that part of his nature which distinguishes him from the rest of the animal world.

It was Charles Darwin who wrote towards the end of his life that among his greatest regrets was the absence of any musical sense or appreciation. When he was young, he said, he had loved music, and the violin in particular. But he had grown so involved in his scientific pursuits that through lack of exercise, his musical sense had atrophied; and coming to an age when he might have enjoyed it, he found it was too late. He could no longer appreciate it, and this lack he lamented as a great loss.

Darwin's story is not unique. Circumstances may vary, but the atrophy of certain of our faculties is self-evident. This may even be true of man's faculty for the divine. On some occasions, as with the artist, the sacred forces its attention upon us. We may, if we are wise, give ourselves time when such a moment occurs. Or we may make the time, preferably regularly, to wait for the Sacred, and find that we are in the presence of God.

II. THE CHURCH TRULY SECULAR

THERE is a world of difference between secularism and secularization. The former suggests a satisfaction with this life in space and time with no desire ever to get away from it; the latter is a process in which an individual or institution acknowledges that existence in the rarefied atmosphere of spiritual contemplation is incomplete and attempts to move into the ordinary life of every day.

That the Church should be involved in everyday life is easier said than done. A number of churches, even by this world's standards, are great institutions, each with its own life and clientele. Such churches demand not only the requisite gifts to keep the plant going, they also need the willing work of those who are prepared to offer their services—for the same reason.

It is hard for a church to change direction. If for years it has had a vested interest in its own continuance, it does not find it easy to lose itself in the service of God in the community.

But to such a life all God's people are called. It demands an immense volume of new thinking and new planning. These have barely begun. It has been customary for years without number for the Church to organize its own activities. Whenever possible its buildings are erected for this purpose. And quite often the vitality of a church is measured by the church organizations it spawns.

And because the local church needs so much help to keep it and its activities going, the more devoted and energetic of its laity will give a vast amount of time outside their working hours to implement the church's programme.

It may well be that at a time when the social services

had not begun, the church was the only institution in the neighbourhood concerned with the needs of its parishioners. It therefore sought to supply their most urgent wants and also provided the fellowship which was lacking to give meaning and hope to otherwise meaningless and hopeless lives.

With the introduction of the Welfare State and the breakdown of class differentiation, as well as with the growth of the trades unions and other workers' associations, these special church agencies are no longer called for. At least not for the same reasons. One of the clearest indications of the change in attitude can be seen in the old University settlements, dotted about the East End of London on both sides of the Thames. Almost without exception, these are struggling to find the right sort of purpose for the nineteen-sixties, and they would be the first to admit that they have not come up with a really effective answer. In some instances they have become hostels or special training centres for students, and in so doing they perform a very useful function. But this is far from the settlement's original intention of serving and being identified with the community where it was built.

The church's difficulties are even more obvious. In the first place, only a handful of people, a very small proportion of the local population, makes a practice of coming to church. For the most part, the church retains the good-will of many thousands, but not their attendance or commitment. And what is true of the church itself is true also of its organizations. Again, only a handful come, made up of people who like the sort of thing the church provides. But, to be honest, only very seldom are they drawn from the most dynamic elements of the community. Of course, it is recognized that the church is useful on certain occasions—a wedding, a baptism, a funeral—and there are times when the Church can speak in favour of somebody who earnestly needs help. But that the Church is concerned with modern life, with urban and commercial living generally, this is seldom taken seriously. People believe that the Church exists for the small group that likes that sort of thing. And that is all there is to it.

Is the Church right to set itself up as a sacred enclave over against the secular world? Is this what the Incarnation was about? If it is honestly resolved to follow Jesus, must it not come down from its high horse, and get itself spattered with mud in the main streets and from the open sewers of the earth?

Surely it will mean that the Church must cease to seal itself off from what happens in the world; on the contrary, its members will go out into the world, there to make the Gospel real by the quality of their lives. It may well be asked if the Church is not doing this already. The average congregation is composed of men and women who, it is true, have to earn their daily bread in the world, and yet who are tempted to regard this as a shadowy kind of life; they really come alive only in the church and its purlieus. In other words, they come alive only in their spare time and at week-ends.

Can we believe that this is how God meant people to live? To be actively concerned for His will during, at the most, a quarter of their waking hours, while the remaining three-quarters they regard as hostile or irrelevant to their Christian discipleship.

This is plainly ridiculous. If we are called to be Christians we are called for twenty-four hours of every day. Christians have no time off. They do not work office hours. And this being so, the Church, which is 'the blessed company of all faithful people', must be engaged in all that makes up man's life in society.

Many people at present are saying that this is the Church's main, and perhaps its only, job. They would hold that there is no effective way in which a believer can show his love for God except by loving his neighbour, and that therefore the service of one's neighbour is all-important. How else, it is said, can a man serve God and show his love for Him? He is more likely to find God in the misery of human beings than in a coterie of respectable people who have gathered to sing hymns and say prayers. Did not our Lord Himself say: 'Inasmuch as ye have done it unto one of the least of these my brethren, ye have done it unto me'? This is the way to serve Christ, to imitate as far as we can our Lord's Incarnation and to identify ourselves with those who suffer and are in need. Jesus has been called 'The Man for Others'. Is this not to be the name too of His followers?

We serve God by serving our neighbour, because our Lord is in our neighbour, and we can never separate Him from the humanity which He has joined to Himself. At the moment of St. Paul's conversion, the words he hears are: 'Saul, Saul, why persecutest thou me?' This can mean nothing else than a union between our Lord and the small bands of early believers; in attacking them Paul was attacking their Lord.

The argument is spelt out in the first Epistle of St. John, where we read: 'If a man say "I love God", and hateth his brother whom he hath seen, how can he love God whom he hath not seen?'. A few sentences earlier the writer makes it even clearer in this bald statement: 'If we love one another, God dwelleth in us, and his love is perfected in us'.

It is a sad fact that the history of the Church fails to put the dedication to the act of love and service first. We are horrified, and rightly horrified, when we learn of the number of crimes against humanity which have been committed in the name of religion. We think with shame of the numerous occasions on which the Church has taken to arms, to enforce what it considers to be orthodoxy. We read with a deep sense of guilt how often Christians have put fellow-Christians to the rack, and even to the stake, because their interpretation of truth was different from that which at the moment has the upper hand. It is a frightful record, and yet it has lingered on in a variety of forms until our own day.

Again and again some ruler, bent on aggression, has invoked the blessing of God on his nefarious exploits, and apparently found no inconsistency between his belief and his behaviour. And this practice is not so out of date as it ought to be.

Is orthodoxy a matter of creed or of conduct? This is not to question the fact that there is a close link between the two, far closer than many are prepared to recognize. As the old saying has it: 'It is not what you think you are; but what you think, you are!' A man's belief will find expression in his actions; but only if his faith is really part of him and not a rendering of lip-service alone.

When his faith is truly alive, he cannot rest satisfied with the average parish programme, which so often draws him away from his responsibilities in the world in order to take part in some specifically church activities. Many of our church buildings over the last century and more have been built with this in mind. And often the church used to run a spate of organizations to interest the old, to enthuse the young, to encourage the mothers and to intrigue the fathers. But, generally, the church plant is no longer used in this way. The centre of community life has moved elsewhere, and the church has been left in a backwater, which sometimes is unpleasantly stagnant. This is not to be bewailed as a sad example of the church's failures and its inability to speak God's word to our contemporaries. It may, in fact, be a mark of the church's success, so that whereas in the past the church was about the only institution offering people some sense of community, of 'belonging', there are now hundreds of bodies doing exactly this thing, and the church, which first taught the community, is therefore often by-passed. Of this by-passing, there is mounting evidence. And the result is that the comparatively few people who still belong to the church find their energies almost impossibly extended to keep a minimum of the church's activities in being and to raise the astronomical sums required to keep the plant from serious deterioration, if not collapse.

It is high time that we grappled with this problem radically. The first question is: what is the function of the local church in the late nineteen-sixties of our era? Are we right in diverting the abilities of a lively group of people to the task of maintaining church buildings, or should we not rather see to it that the Church—not as a building, but as a group of people—is penetrating the life of the area in which they live, and is serving our Lord by putting into practice His 'Inasmuch . . .'? This will demand of the faithful a readiness to be involved in politics, trades unions, race relations, social services and, indeed, all that makes up a present day community.

A phrase, much in use, is that the Church to be the Church at all, must be a *caring* Church, and it is stated that only a church which gives itself to the service of its neighbourhood has any right to the name. Its care will, of course, extend beyond its local area, and there may well be national or world movements in which it feels it right to engage.

If the Church begins to live like this, it is unlikely that it will want to go on using its plant for the accustomed 'churchly' purposes. There is absolutely no doubt that the maintenance of many of these buildings has become an almost insupportable burden around the neck of the incumbent and of the few who are willing to share it with him. If, however, the buildings can be used for the benefit of the community generally, this particular burden may be greatly lightened, thus releasing both the incumbent and his close helpers for the work waiting to be done in the neighbourhood.

There are already many examples of this—some church halls are used as clinics, others for nursery education; and some have crypts which, even in these days, are used for the homeless or for drug-addicts. Does this not sound better than a round of meetings of the faithful in the halls, often issuing in no action at all but a request to come again and to bring somebody with you? What is wrong with this 'church as a building' attitude is basically that it is a plea for Christians to go back to the catacombs, instead of a recognition of the Church as the herald of the Kingdom of God. There can be no abrogation of social responsibility. The call to the Church is no different from that to the individual : 'If any man will come after me', says Jesus, 'let him deny himself and take up his cross and follow me'. The Church, too, must be willing to die in order to live. A death to a great deal of prestige and historical grandeur and sentimental affection, and also to long-accepted customs, in order that it may live triumphantly and relevantly in the changing order of our time.

When Jesus told His disciples : 'Ye are in the world, but not of the world', He was surely telling them that their work was to infiltrate and penetrate the world but to be on their guard that they were not absorbed by it.

Penetration not absorption is the way of obedience.

Moreover it has to be remembered that the Church is bigger than the members who compose it, and in consequence the Church can speak to society in a more responsible manner than any individual. I realize that I am writing in ideal terms. We all know to our shame how again and again in history many a reform has been pushed through in the face of the Church's hostility. Nevertheless the Church is the conscience of the community. Sometimes it warns; sometimes it challenges; often it leads, and sometimes it encourages. There will also be occasions when it pioneers some new social venture in the name of Christ which eventually, when public opinion has been sufficiently stirred, is taken over by the civic authorities, leaving the Church free to take some further step in Christ's service. But mainly it trains its people to take active responsibility in the ordinary on-going life of society.

Certainly the Church must cease to be an institution, interested primarily in its own continuance. Certainly its members must express the reality of their faith in God by the service of their fellowmen. Certainly it needs to be secularized without becoming secular. But together with all this it must remain the means whereby men are fed with the Word of God and the Bread of Life. It must remain the vehicle God uses to declare His Word to humanity. It must help people to 'study to be quiet' rather than always rushing aimlessly about. It must, in other words, maintain the validity of the sacred in a world which more and more thinks it can do without it.

III. THE CHURCH FULLY SACRED

THE argument of this book is that the sacred and the secular must be brought together again. The author believes passionately in the Church's mission in the ordinary world of space and time, and he holds no brief for a segregated community which seeks to cultivate its own garden while leaving the rest of the world unsown by the Word of God. On the other hand, he does not favour a Church which loses its uniqueness by trying to come to terms with the world in a way which suggests it is no more than an effective machine in the hands of social workers. He would hold that Christianity parts company with Humanism, not because He believes that the things which Humanism stands for are wrong, but because he believes that Humanism does not go far enough. A Church which thinks itself exclusively an instrument in the hands of those who have a conscience about the present state of the world is inadequate to meet the deepest needs of the human personality. Man needs more than to be clothed and housed and fed.

There is a famine of the Spirit which may well be the major problem of those who live in the affluent society of the West. And this may be neither ignored nor disregarded. Either man is an exceptionally well-developed animal, but nothing more than an animal; or there is a basic difference between man and the rest of the animal creation as a result of which man is able to get into touch with the eternal. If the latter is true then time and opportunity must be found for the training and development of the sacred part of human personality.

Not that man should be cut up into separate water-tight compartments. He is all of a piece, and if he is a truly rounded, a whole and healthy, i.e. a holy, human being, his emphasis on the sacred will be seen to be as real an element in his constitution as his emphasis on the secular. These two must not be set over against each other; they are entirely complementary. The secular is truncated apart from the sacred; the sacred is diminished apart from the secular.

Our Lord came to this world to help people *to be* and not just *to do*. We in the West know the mad rush in which we live; we shrug our shoulders as if there were no escape. The well-known quotation hits us hard: 'What you are speaks so loud that I cannot hear what you say'. The Church must give us the time we need to recollect our souls, to be found of Christ and to find ourselves in Him, to learn what Père de Caussade called 'the sacrament of the present moment', and to realize that eternity impinges on every moment of our lives.

The necessary secularization of the Church is not the whole story. The Church's involvement in everything that makes up life in the neighbourhood does not call for complete absorption, so that those who are Christian grow increasingly indistinguishable from those who are not. By his incorporation into Christ, the Christian lives partly in a new dimension, the dimension of eternity. This part of him needs to be fed and nourished and the affairs of this world should not demand his attention to such an extent that the 'sacred' part of him is in danger of being crushed to death.

The Church must never lose its identity in its service of the world, otherwise why did Christ found it? It has a sacred function as the Church *vis-à-vis* the world, which may not be surrendered. One of the most important of these is to look after the believers. The truth is that most of us are not strong enough to stand on our own feet without a regular re-charging of our spiritual batteries. It may be questioned why the heroic experiment concerning the worker priests in France was brought to an end, and there is no doubt a number of valid answers. But one reason given was that the priests were infected by the atmosphere in which they lived and lost the essentially 'sacred' element in their ministry. Do not most of us know something of this danger?

Those who live in situations uncongenial to Christianity need special grace to keep themselves 'unspotted from the world'. This was very clear in South Africa. If a priest had the good fortune to leave the country regularly, he remained alert to the wickedness of the policy of *apartheid*. But if circumstances reduced such opportunities to a minimum, sooner or later he would catch the poisonous infection with a resultant blurring of the clarity of his vision.

So it is that Christians in the New Testament are told not to forsake 'the assembling of themselves together'; and the believers, as the Acts has it, continued in the Apostles' teaching, in the Fellowship, in the Breaking of Bread and in the Prayers. This New Testament Quadrilateral has never been rescinded; and though it does not call for elaborate church buildings (or even church buildings at all) it insists that there must be regular occasions when Christians meet, in order to worship God, to be instructed in the Faith, to share in the Eucharist and to experience the reality of the divine Fellowship. If any of these is missing, the residue is no true church at all, and those who belong to it go forward sadly incomplete.

We must not gloss over the perils.

It is undoubtedly true that there are still many priests and other ministers of religion who think of the Church almost exclusively in institutional terms. Although frequently they are men who emphasize the sacredness of their calling, and who are quick to draw the skirts of their cassocks back from the mud thrown up by a passing lorry or from any other mundane contamination, they are in fact, though quite unintentionally, adopting a completely secular attitude towards religion. Not an attitude of infiltration and penetration, but an attitude of secularism in which profit and loss are measured strictly in the currency of this world. Men such as these are apt to think that if at the end of the year the accounts balance and the number of communicants has increased, the Kingdom of God has come. This is a quantitative judgment which equates the Church with any ordinary human association and spells death to the eternal reality of the Church and to any opportunity of Christian advance.

This is not to say that people should not be encouraged to come to church, or that the church should not try to be self-supporting financially. But it is not surprising that when this point of view is over emphasized, young believers with a more heroic and costly conception of their Faith convince themselves that there is no way forward but by the death of the Church as an institution and its rebirth in small unofficial groups of men and women who meet informally to strengthen themselves in their faith and to be encouraged in their witness.

The truth is that the break-up of the Church as we know it is neither likely nor desirable. Practically speaking, far too many secular interests are involved in its existence to permit its disappearance; and there must be centres to which people can come where the Word of God is preached and the Sacraments duly administered. In pastoral terms, there are still thousands upon thousands of people to whom their church means everything. This is true of the Victorian Gothic structures in our conurbations; it is equally true of our villages, where the church still plays an important part in the community, though considerably and tragically less since the days of the non-resident parson. He may well be living five or six miles away, and the smallness of the benefice incomes in these days of inflation compel his Bishop to make him the parish priest of three or four villages. As a result he cannot really be the parson of the parish.

But we should be giving a false picture of the situation if we did not recognize the large part the local 'man of God' can still play in the community. The days when people touched their forelocks to him as being God's representative in the parish as well as socially superior to most of the parishioners are well and truly over. He now has to find his place by his own qualities. He will be asked to share in many of the local activities and pursuits, and there will be welfare agencies and organizations eager to enlist his services. How far he joins in all these opportunities is for him to decide—on his knees.

The parishioners do not basically want a social worker, however well-trained; that is to say they do not want their parson to be that social worker. They want him to be (without quotes this time) their man of God who carries them and all their needs on his heart, who leads their worship whether they themselves are present or not, who offers the Holy Eucharist on their behalf, and who is their 'guide, philosopher and friend'. Sooner or later the time comes that the dam bursts, and a parishioner is overwhelmed by his own spiritual bankruptcy; then he needs to be able to confide in the man he knows who has been set apart for sacred things.

One of the facts of the spiritual life which every priest must learn is the sacrament of personality. I can well remember the release that came to me when the Gospel ceased to depend on a subjective appreciation of it, and I learnt to understand that it had an objective reality apart altogether from my feelings. It in no sense depended on me or the quality of my faith; it depended entirely on Christ's redemptive action on behalf of all humanity.

This was a liberation; and as a priest I received great comfort from the old ecclesiastical tag: *ex opere operato.* That is to say, the effectiveness of a priest's actions does not derive from his own holiness of life but from the indelible marks of priesthood with which he was sealed at his Ordination. This I still thankfully believe; and nothing in nearly forty years in the Sacred Ministry has done anything to weaken that conviction; the success or otherwise of a man's ministry is due to God's action, not his own ability or sanctity.

For the last fifteen years I have been a Bishop, with all the oversight the episcopal calling entails, and the hard school of experience has taught me that a man's personality must not be disregarded, either for good or for harm. God has given us His treasure 'in earthen vessels', and these vessels are not mass produced. Each one is different. Each one is signed by its Maker. And each one by its very nature is sacramental—it is an outward and visible sign of the Divine Grace within it. Why is it that one incumbent visits his people assiduously, prepares his sermons unhurriedly and faithfully, is quick to attend the bedside of anyone who is sick, and yet, humanly speaking, fails to evoke any obvious response from the parishioners? The next door parish is fortunate in having a similarly dedicated priest, but, in addition, he has a gift of imagination, a gift of friendship, some indefinable flair, perhaps, which all combine to awaken general interest so that people come from far and near to attend his services. This is humanly inexplicable, but its truth is beyond doubt.

As the apostle Paul wrote: 'Behold I show you a mystery'; and this sacrament of personality is one of which everyone must take heed, be he bishop, priest or layman. We are all so pachydermatous that this is a subject which calls for prayer and fasting, and also for painstaking study and research. What could be better than if in its School of Theology, every University was to establish a Chair of Pastoral Responsibility, occupied by a professor with extensive pastoral experience, and with the capacity to inspire enthusiasm and application in his students?

But though St. Paul wrote: 'Behold I show you a mystery', he went on to say: 'but we shall all be changed'. In spite of all our ignorance we can hold on to our faith in the Divine Power, which can turn weakness into strength, and provide grace sufficient for every need. Irrespective of anything else that cries to be done, we must so give ourselves to God's service and the doing of His will that the 'earthen vessels', lay as well as clerical, without losing a fraction of the earthiness that is the glory of their creation, become lenses rather than shades. No longer shall they conceal the light of Christ, but instead they shall focus and direct it to those situations where it is patently needed.

The Church believes that it is a divine creation. Not necessarily exactly in its present form; nevertheless it holds that within the New Covenant it is in Christ the heir and descendant of the chosen people of the Old Covenant. Its appointment is an essential part of God's redemptive activity in Christ, sacred in character, and differing from all other human assemblies in that it is an organism before it is an organization. But as the single cell has to discover the purpose of its being within the human body, so the individual believer achieves significance within the Body of Christ. It can be maintained that there is no Christian apart from the Church, and even the castaway on a desert island, though he may have to practise his faith in isolation, is still a Christian by reason of his incorporation in the Church of God.

To the Church, our Lord issued His command to preach the Gospel to all men. How this is to be done, and the organization to do it, may vary from place to place; but that it must be done, of this there is no question. As a result, the world over, there are houses of God and houses of Prayer, set apart for the worship of God, instruction in righteousness and the preaching of the Gospel.

Nothing in our contemporary situation suggests that this should come to an end. It must be remembered there is nothing sacrosanct about the traditional church plant, composed of a building for worship, a hall or halls for activities organized by the church, and a parsonage. Indeed, as has already been noted, some of these may be far too elaborate to meet the requirements of our day. *En passant* it ought to be remembered that the building associated in people's minds with the well-known if unused pattern of church worship is not normally the best place to proclaim the evangel. Many people are loth to go into a church because they feel that in doing so they are aligning themselves with a way of life which either does not interest them or with which they are at the moment unready to identify themselves. However the Gospel is to be declared in our day, it is unlikely that it will be heard by the un-evangelized until use is made of neutral rather than church buildings.

Nevertheless, unless we believe the Church should be a gathered community, that is to say, it should be a perfectionist group of believers, it is generally held that there ought to be services of worship to which all may come. The act of worship is open to all, though some parts of it will be restricted to those who accept the Church's discipline. As in the Church of England, there may be an insistence on Confirmation before Communion—at least in usual circumstances. But the emphasis is on the open church. It is there for all the parishioners and available to all who wish to use it.

Yet, in the long history of the Church, evidence of an overwhelming kind indicates very clearly that renewal has come through quite small bodies of people who have banded themselves together in lives of fellowship and determined obedience to the Lord. This is as true of the monastic movement as of their Methodist class meeting. This century too has seen its cell-movement and other bodies working with the minimum of organization such as the Servants of Christ the King. As long ago as the New Testament period this looks to have been the pattern for advance. Our Lord chose twelve men 'that they might be with him and that he might send them forth'. And even from this hand-picked dozen, He carefully chose three for special instruction and responsibility. As Bishop Wand reminded us in his Lent Book for 1967, they were the ones who went with our Lord both to the Mount of Transfiguration and to the Garden of Gethsemane.

No sensible person will offer easy prophecies for the future; but history recommends the growth of devoted nuclei of people in all areas—Christians who really take their faith seriously, and who dedicate themselves to serve their Lord as faithfully as they know in all that makes up their lives. They will be on their guard against separating themselves from the larger church of the neighbourhood, but they must be given the opportunity of challenging and strengthening fellowship. This cannot be provided in a church community which has to make provision at the same time for people at all stages of spiritual development. It may be that many small fellowships will grow up in a single parish, each brought together first of all by a specific concern of its own. And in these ecumenical days, these fellowships may well jump across the still existing denominational barriers and begin to give shape to the Great Church of the future which is all our longing and our prayer.

In the jargon of to-day it needs to be emphasized that these fellowships must be open-ended fellowships—constantly growing, constantly changing, constantly proliferating. Only so can they be saved from growing into introverted groups or mutual admiration societies. Their outward looking and continuous progress is a crucially important part of the parish priest's work, and affords one of the reasons why the local 'man of God' is still urgently needed.

It is in ways such as these that the Church of the nineteen-sixties will begin to resemble more closely the Apostolic Church of the New Testament when, as a result of their continuance in the New Testament Quadrilateral, the Lord added to them daily such as were being saved.

One of the clearest signs of the sacred nature of our Faith is to be found in the Sacraments. In their use the believer takes part in an action outside the terms of reference of the exact sciences. To the anti-religious mind, he is taking part in a form of primitive magic, and no more. But let him be on his guard; it is not so long ago that matter was believed to have substantial reality. Now it is known to consist of energy, and matter as such is no more.

It is worth recalling that in its sacraments, the Church uses the common things of life—oil, water, wine and bread. These were the things with which everyone in the Holy Land was in touch, and were to be found in the simplest peasant's home.

In the Sacraments our Lord released, as it were, not only the physical but the spiritual energy within them. And in so doing, He revealed that the whole of creation was shot through by the Spirit of God. Charles Davis in his little book makes much of the difference between the sacred and the secular and makes many valuable points for his purpose. But too sharp a dichotomy between the secular and the sacred can unhappily result in a blatant isolationism on either side while insisting on autonomy in its own sphere and ignoring the other.

While it is right that Christians should lose themselves in the service of their fellows, their purpose is not to go into the world as a group of 'do gooders', *de haut en bas*. In the Spirit of the Eucharist he recognizes that the believer, as much as the unbeliever, is involved in all that makes up ordinary existence : he has to earn his living; he is part of his family ; he is caught up in the political ebb and flow of his country; and he has responsibilities to the nation of which he is a citizen. This is the general picture. There may be a very tiny proportion whose vocation it is to witness to the reality of the sacred, by withdrawing from the secular world into a nunnery or monastery. But all have to work out the significance of the Incarnation for themselves, and most in the ordinary life of every day.

Their concern for life in the world must be no assumed attitude. Our Lord never questions the reality of all that makes up human existence here and now. He teaches His disciples to pray : 'Thy kingdom come, thy will be done ; on earth as it is in heaven' ; and He institutes the Sacraments to strengthen those disciples. It is true that 'here we have no continuing city', but while we are here we try to prepare the world for the coming of its King. The Christian approach to the world is two-pronged ; on the one hand we share in its failures, its strivings and its weaknesses by reason of our humanity ; on the other, by reason of our share in Christ's redemptive work, we are to express the love and the will of God in the tangled web of relationships, many of which find corporate as well as personal expression, not directed to human beings only but to the whole of creation. This last is not to be excluded; it embraces our treatment of the animals over whom man has been given dominion, and of the land and the water as revealed to us in such a new science as ecology.

Christians are therefore to be found in any walk of life in which a man can work not only for his own sustenance and that of his family, but also for the well-being of society —both long and short-term. This is not to say that he will not lend his energies to philanthropic and charitable causes, or that he will not do those 'works of mercy', as they used to be called, when occasion is given. It is, in fact, reasonable to suppose that Christians will figure prominently in these, if for no other reason than that, because he does not fix his goal within this life, he will be less concerned about the material return than those who put all their eggs into this world's basket!

Nor should it occasion surprise that a believer whose faith leads him to particular concern with relationships, should be quick to assess areas of human need and do his best to meet them and where necessary to set up agencies to work for their amelioration. But, let it be repeated, in all this there must be no smell of condescension. Those who recall the splendid film entitled 'M. Vincent' about St. Vincent de Paul may be reminded of one of its closing shots. The saint, now an old man and almost on his death-bed, is instructing one of the probationers in the Order which he had founded. Very wisely, he says to her: 'Never forget that in dispensing charity it is very hard not to breed resentment in the person to whom you give it'. We want no recurrence of the Lady Bountifuls who went among the poor to do good for an hour or two a day, and returned to their own comfortable homes in the evening!

The sacramental life of the Church is thus of tremendous significance, for every Sacrament validly celebrated is an earnest of the fact that there is to be not only a new heaven but also a new earth. 'The whole creation groaneth and travaileth in pain together until now.' But there is a promise of cosmic renewal. As matter has given place to energy, so energy will give place to Spirit. The Sacraments ensure our taking the physical world seriously, and therefore our treating it reverently, in that they reveal its potential in the purpose of God. They help to capture the world for God. Which means that the world fundamentally is more than rational; it is sacred. Which is why the worshipping life of the Church must go on.

No lesson is more important for our generation. Perhaps it comes home to us most simply in the words addressed to St. Peter on the roof-top in Joppa: 'What God has cleansed, call thou not uncommon or unclean'.

IV. THE MATERIAL UNIVERSE?

THERE is something strangely ironical about the enthusiastic secularization of the Church at a time in world history when men of science have left behind them a materialistic view of the universe. One could have understood it far more easily a hundred years ago, when religion was being forced to retreat before the growth of the scientific temper, and in any argument the spokesmen for the Church, almost invariably basing their convictions on false premises, were defeated over and over again by the secularists of the time.

To-day there is a completely changed attitude. This is not a scientific treatise, but the humblest layman scanning the world of the physicist and the astronomer is left in no doubt that the old materialism has been utterly rejected. The table I am sitting at as I type these words, the typewriter itself, and the paper I am using, have in common that not only are they material things, but that the material of which they are made can be broken down ultimately to impulses of energy. In fact the whole world, indeed the whole universe, is composed of energy. The molecules and atoms of the past which were the foundation of a materialistic science have themselves been resolved into the electrons, neutrons and protons of the twentieth century.

If we try to state this fact in religious terms, we dare to say that this ultimate energy differs not at all from the creative Spirit of Faith. The secret of the universe lies in this Spirit-Energy, which Christians have been as slow to recognize as have the scientists. And with less excuse. One of the very first verses of the Bible tells us that the world was created by God : the Scriptures develop the conviction that the Holy Spirit was the means by which that creation was accomplished and remains the means by which the creation is sustained and goes on from day to day.

In the chaos out of which God made the world, we read
that the Spirit of God hovered over the face of the form-
less waters. In our belief in the Unity of the Trinity, it is
seldom profitable to attempt to isolate in detail the work
of the Father from that of the Son and that again from the
Holy Spirit. But to get the Biblical Revelation as straight as
we can, we ought to say that the Son was the Father's effective agent in the creation, and the Spirit was and still is the
means by which it is accomplished.

St. Paul, in his letter to the Colossians, lays down plainly
the Scriptural belief. I quote from the Jerusalem Bible
(Col. 1 : 15–20):

> Christ is the image of the unseen God
> and the first-born of all creation,
> for in him were created
> all things in heaven and on earth :
> everything visible and everything invisible,
> Thrones, Dominations, Sovereignties, Powers—
> all things were created through him and for him.
> Before anything was created, he existed,
> and he holds all things in unity.
> Now the Church is his body,
> he is its head.
>
> As he is the Beginning,
> he was the first to be born from the dead,
> so that he should be first in every way ;
> because God wanted all perfection
> to be found in him
> and all things to be reconciled through him and for him,
> everything in heaven and everything on earth,
> when he made peace
> by his death on the cross.

In a valuable footnote to this passage, the editors say :
' . . . it seems likely that the reference here is to the biblical
concept of the entire cosmos as filled with the creative

D

presence of God', and they go on: 'Paul teaches that the incarnation and resurrection make Christ head not only of the entire human race, but of the entire created cosmos, so that everything that was involved in the fall is equally involved in the salvation'.

In a statement like the one just quoted, the apostle is formulating no new doctrine, particularly so far as God's creative activity is concerned. Though it is true that the consummation of all things in Christ as the fruit of His redemption may be held to be the essentially new Christian revelation, it springs from the belief in God's creation, which rendered imperfect by the fall (which is the technical expression to signify the entry of pain and evil into the world) is restored to its original perfection through Christ's atoning work in His life and death and resurrection. We find this belief in its completest—and most mysterious form—in St. Paul's letter to the Romans in which he writes:

> The whole creation is eagerly waiting for God to reveal his sons. It was not for any fault on the part of creation that it was made unable to attain its purpose, it was made so by God; but creation still retains the hope of being freed, like us, from its slavery to decadence, to enjoy the same freedom and glory as the children of God. From the beginning till now the entire creation, as we know, has been groaning in one great act of giving birth; and not only creation, but all of us who possess the firstfruits of the Spirit, we too groan inwardly as we wait for our bodies to be set free (Romans 8: 18–23).

This is uncompromising language, and belief in the divine activity throughout all creation is Scriptural through and through. The psalmist sings over and over again in almost similar words that the whole earth is full of God's glory. The same thought recurs in the prophetic writings (e.g. Isaiah 6:3 and Jeremiah 23:24), and it is explicitly repeated throughout the Wisdom literature. In the 42nd chapter of Ecclesiasticus there is a magnificent sequence which tells of God's glory and activity in Nature :

By the words of the Lord his works come into being
and all creation obeys his will.
As the sun in shining looks on all things,
so the work of the Lord is full of his glory.
The Lord has not granted to the holy ones
to tell of all his marvels
which the Almighty Lord has solidly constructed
for the universe to stand firm in his glory . . .

He has imposed an order on the magnificent works of his wisdom,
he is from everlasting to everlasting,
nothing can be added to him, nothing taken away,
he needs no one's advice. How desirable are all his works,
how dazzling to the eye !
They all live and last for ever,
whatever the circumstances all obey him.
All things go in pairs, by opposites,
and he has made nothing defective ;
the one consolidates the excellence of the other,
who could ever be sated with gazing at his glory?

A little later in the 43rd chapter, these remarkable words occur :

Thanks to him all ends well,
and all things hold together by means of his word.

According to the editors of the Jerusalem Bible the Book of Wisdom takes over a phrase from the Stoic vocabulary to emphasize the function of the Spirit of the Lord which maintains the cosmos in unity. It runs thus :

The spirit of the Lord, indeed, fulfils the whole world,
and that which holds all things together knows every word that is said.

This fundamentally religious meaning of matter was over

the centuries more and more neglected by the Church, so much so that a false dividing wall was built between the sacred and the secular, which is still having its bitter consequences to-day. That there is a sphere where the secular has its own discipline and authority is not to be questioned. Our Lord made this transparently clear when He said: 'Render unto Caesar the things which are Caesar's and unto God the things which are God's'. In the course of history only very seldom has there been any danger of humanity's rendering unto God the things that belong to Caesar, but all too often it has rendered unto Caesar the things that are God's.

This is not to deny, as the Bible underlines, that there is in society a secular arm which, so long as it does not trespass on God's preserve, is entitled to obedience and respect. St. Paul, for most of his life, showed no hesitation in calling in the help of the State to defend him against his enemies. Though it was not a religious institution, he recognized it as being God-given and accepted it as the legitimate secular authority. But the State, when it arrogates to itself divine authority and prerogative, is a blasphemous 'anti-Christ' which must be resisted at all costs. His refusal to accept this attitude was the final cause of Paul's execution. As the Book of the Revelation explains again and again, the state becomes abhorrent as it assumes a religious status. It is by nature secular, having its own secular autonomy; in seeking a 'religious' allegiance, it oversteps its ordained limitations (very much after the pattern of the fall of man) and attempts to take to itself a sacred function, which is not Christian but diabolical.

What emerges plainly from the Bible is that there is an order of Law and an order of Grace, each with its own proper province and responsibility. But while this is true of humanity, it does not follow that it is true of Nature as a whole. Humanity is in a unique position. God has given to man the right to choose. He does not ooze unconsciously into the Kingdom of God. Through Christ's atonement he can, if he will, move from bondage to sin to the liberty of salvation. When the State is run by Christian men honestly seeking to be true to their Lord in their decisions they will not seek to extend the State's authority beyond its given limits, and at the same time they will give it a moral and even a sacred function.

It would be quite wrong to save the idea of the sacred for that which is inexplicable in scientific terms. Obviously, the man who is an out-and-out secularist will choose to regard the scientific explanation as all-sufficient. So far as he is concerned, there is no inclination to look beyond what he can assess and understand; and he can support his attitude by steadfastly refusing to look any further. So it is that many people to-day accept the existence of the universe without question. True, year by year it is revealing more of its secrets and the exploration of outer space is penetrating ever more deeply into the boundless distances measured in light-years. But there are equally many whose minds cannot stop short of the question which asks how did all this begin and how is it sustained. One can deliberately exclude this as an unwelcome intrusion into scientific theory and experiment; but it could well be held that the person who never seriously poses this question is failing to give expression to the fullness of his manhood. This is asking for no obscurantist outlook; on the contrary, it is obscurantist to disregard it. A century ago the secularist could properly play the ball into the believer's court. Now, equally properly the ball can be sent back into his.

Nor is it only the mystery of the universe's beginnings and present continuance. In addition man has to choose whether there is a goal towards which the whole creation moves—which is what Teilhard de Chardin was never tired of writing—or whether, though he believes in man's evolution to a higher order of being, this is due to blind chance. It ought to be stressed that spelling 'nature' with a capital N is the coward's way of evading either faith or decision.

There is an heroic element in Christian faith which cannot be ignored. In the face of the measureless tragedy and cruelty in the world, it seems incredibly foolhardy to assert that God is Love. But so far as the believer is concerned, he says with Martin Luther: 'Here I stand; I can do no other'. In spite of all the world has to offer in terms of pain and sorrow, he believes that God has revealed Himself most clearly to man in Jesus Christ. Not only in what He said, but also in what He did. The effects of His redemptive work are still continuing. Just as a doctor values his patient's pain as a means to diagnosis and cure, so God uses man's grief and frustration as a way forward to that new heaven and new earth which will renew and transform the cosmos as we know it. The ultimate mystery is not knowledge but love.

There are many ways of looking at the world around us. At a chamber concert the member of the audience who embraces in his own musical interests the making of violins will listen in a particular manner which does not appeal to the ordinary music lover and concert goer. The scientist who is professionally concerned with the whole realm of sound will in his turn give the concert his specialized attention—though this is not to suggest that the scientist may not become a concert goer who forgets his technical concerns from time to time, and who surrenders himself completely to the music being performed.

The doctor generally looks at the human body from an anatomical point of view. The artist regards it quite differently, though with the examples of Leonardo and Michelangelo, he is aware that anatomical knowledge ought to be added to his artistic vision.

When outsiders discuss two young people in love, we have all heard the expression : 'I can't think what he sees in her', or, 'in him'. And for that matter the passion that draws a man and a woman together when they are nineteen years old is very different from their mature affection when they are fifty-nine.

And so it goes on : the vision of the mystic and the vision of the lover, the vision of the doctor and of the artist ; that of the scientist contrasted with that of the music lover. It can be multiplied over and over again. To a quite considerable extent we can learn to put ourselves into other people's shoes so that *their* reactions become genuinely our own.

In the present age, the high priest of humanity is the man of science, and science is the god to be worshipped. But, from time to time, people arise who show us convincingly that this prevalent attitude is not the only one—not even the only one that is respectable. Any number of people in this technological period are glad that out of their own experience they can say 'Amen' to Elizabeth Barrett Browning's well-known words :

> Earth's crammed with heaven,
>   And every common bush aflame with God ;
> But only he who sees takes off his shoes :
>   The rest just sit around it and pluck blackberries.

Modern science, with its forthright rejection of nineteenth century materialism, has brought to the men and women of to-day a vastly increased knowledge which at the same time is a vastly increased and acknowledged ignorance. Modern science which began by expelling the sacred has brought it back more strongly than ever before.

V. THE LIFE OF FAITH (1)

In honesty we have to admit that the Church is a very mixed institution. There are those who wish it to dispose of all its institutional organization. Then there are those who, rightly in my estimation, want to see the Church getting its priorities right, invading the real world where ordinary people live and move and have their being. They believe that the function of the Church is to be the herald of the Kingdom of God, and that in any appreciable sense the local congregation is to be the foretaste of that Kingdom. It is, in one of Dr. Moffatt's undying phrases, a 'colony of heaven' (Philippians 3:20). Thirdly, there are those who think primarily in institutional terms. Though often unaware of it, they think of the Church as a Christian ghetto, a fall-out shelter for Christians in which they can live their own religious lives in isolation from the world.

The interesting fact is that all or any of these can be completely secularized; equally they can all in various degrees reveal the reality of the sacred. In Otto's famous classic, *The Idea of the Holy,* already referred to and largely pre-Freudian in outlook, he makes it clear that the unveiling of the *Mysterium Tremendum* is unpredictable, and may confront a man anywhere—in church or out of church, in an outward-looking congregation or in one that is concerned exclusively with itself and its own pious interests.

And this is true to our experience. In the course of the last few years, I have been to churches in England where I have been shocked by the lifelessness and the atmosphere of an act of worship which has been no more than a weekly routine performance. Where this attitude unfortunately prevails, I have had to admit that I should never normally go to that church if I were not a 'professional' Christian;

even more so, I should never dare to take an acquaintance whom I was trying to win for the Christian faith—very likely he would be put off for life!

Happily by contrast, I have been to other churches, often with no architectural or artistic aids, where every word and action on the part of both minister and congregation have conveyed the reality of God and the assurance that they are meeting in His presence and for His glory. Unless there is this sense of the numinous, there is little or no point in going to any church at all—however institutional and traditional or however *avant-garde*. That last sentence needs a qualification. In the end of the day we do not go to church for our own sakes but to praise God and because we are enjoined to go. Hence, if we would be obedient Christians we shall continue to go and we shall pray that God in His mercy and His grace will use us to bring into the worshipping community some of the spiritual vitality which is unhappily lacking. Not for any virtue we possess but because of His faithfulness.

The same is to be found with people as with congregations. There are numbers of church-goers we know—perhaps among whom we ourselves ought to be numbered—who convey in their normal workaday lives nothing of the reality of the Eternal. They may go through the right Christian motions, be regular in their church attendance, in saying their prayers, in reading the Scriptures and in partaking of the Sacraments; and one has no reason to doubt that they perform these acts sincerely from a sense of obligation and obedience, yet their religious experience fails to come alive for anybody else.

Others there are, thank God, whose spiritual exercises have so obviously transported them to the courts of heaven that when we meet them, there is still the smell of heaven on their clothes and its radiant glow on their faces. These are the men and women for whom the Pauline title of 'saints' reads particularly appropriately. No longer is it exclusively associated in our minds with figures in stained glass windows, usually wearing haloes and completely disconnected from the happenings of this world except in so far as their sufferings for the Christian cause add to their beatific, not to say smug, expressions. Not at all! These are the sort of people we meet every day doing ordinary manual or professional jobs, and yet who manage to carry about with them a convincing conception of the presence of God, infectious in its quality.

There is no question that their lives have been transformed by their faith. We are not asking that all devout believers should be copy-book imitations of the ideal Scout who is always cheerful and whistles maddeningly under all difficulties. All the same, there are certain marks of the Christian which we have a right to expect. We have a right to assume that he will be unselfish, putting God's glory first and the needs of other men before his own. We have a right to assume that he will not be eaten up by self-pity or jealousy. We are entitled to think that his life will not be consumed by conceit or that he will not suffer from hurt feelings. We do not expect a faithful Christian to be arrogant in his manner or the slave of his passions. We find that his priorities are not the same as those of the average independent man of our time. We are rightly surprised if he is a chain-smoker and his fingers are indelibly—apparently—stained with nicotine. We can surely take it for granted that he will do everything in his power to make his home a happy home which is noticeably set alight by the Divine Presence, and where it is easy to laugh.

We have pretty well a duty as well as a right to suspect a man who does not enjoy being alive, and whose hardly pressed lips convey a censorious and disapproving attitude to life. Of one thing there can be no question, that where the Sacred breaks in, a man reveals beyond all doubt that he is living not under law but under Grace. This is the kind of life which responds to the Divine initiative, in fact, a life which produces the promised fruit of the Spirit: Love, Joy, Peace, Patience, Gentleness, Goodness, Meekness, Faithfulness and Self-control. For all the external changes in man's life over the last two thousand years, there is nothing to suggest that he is not basically the same creature as he was. Unregenerate man exhibits the same selfish qualities as he did at the beginning of the Christian era, and man who has been born again should surely be an exemplar of those qualities which bring home to the bystander the reality of our Lord Jesus Christ. His life must be in the process of being transformed by his genuine but unassuming contact with and experience of the Supernatural.

The fact of the matter is that we dare scarcely believe this. We have grown so impatient of any form of hypocrisy and so accustomed to attributing doubtful motives to almost any action however altruistic, that we have so lost the taste for goodness that we no longer see it. With the result that we excuse ourselves nearly everything and tend to quench any impulses either to be, or to do, good.

It is now a number of years ago that Dorothy Sayers, properly wearied of the Church's blinkered preoccupation with sexual sin, wrote an essay aptly named *The Six Other Deadly Sins*. These six were Pride, Covetousness, Envy, Gluttony, Anger and Sloth. Far too little has been made of their corrupting power. They are entitled to much more attention than they receive and each has extensive ramifications. Yet, it may be that the time has come to think not only of these but of *The Seven Other Deadly Sins* which do so much to stifle the faintly flickering spiritual life.

These would surely include Malicious Gossip, Professional Superficiality (the priest's particular temptation), Self-Pity, Cruelty—in word as much as in deed, Imputation of unworthy motives to others, Heresy Hunting in any form, and inconsiderate Ambition. This is not meant as a final list and everybody can make their own.

Nor does it need underlining that one of the main failures from which the world is suffering to-day is man's lack of concern for, and indifference to, the crying needs of his neighbour. And it can be strongly argued that man's fundamental wish to serve his brother is much harder to foster and to conserve if there is no controlling belief in men and women as ends, ends in themselves, so that they may never be manipulated as means to ends other than their own fulfilment. It is hard to hold on to such a conviction unless man seeks to serve Christ in his brother-man and unless he recognizes that all men are brothers for whom Christ died. In other words, unless you love God your determination to love your neighbour as yourself is dangerously weakened and diminished.

What it comes to is this. Though the Christian and the unbelieving Humanist will find a common concern for mankind generally and for their neighbour in particular, yet there is a special quality of life which the Christian experiences because he is a Christian—because his eyes are opened on the uplands of eternity. If their lives do not witness to this truth, more shame to them!

There are few Christians who have their eyes open all the time. Normally, the hard facts of this world are so much with them as to crowd out the view of the celestial mountains. But from time to time the reality of the eternal forces itself on their consciousness. Suddenly, for no outwardly apparent reason, the common bush is seen to be alight with God. Suddenly man discovers his point of highest development is reached when he recognizes himself as a worshipping animal. Generally this heightened awareness is accompanied by an overwhelming conviction of his own unworthiness, his own uncleanness in comparison with the unstained purity of the Divine. Isaiah cries: 'Woe is me! for I am undone: because I am a man of unclean lips, and I dwell in the midst of a people of unclean lips: for mine eyes have seen the King, the Lord of hosts'. Simon Peter overcome by Jesus' power and presence, cries: 'Depart from me, for I am a sinful man, O Lord'.

Unless some such encounter is ours, even though very infrequently, we have not really been awakened to the reality of the numinous. It is true that this experience cannot be ensured or repeated at will. We cannot guarantee the vision but we can make the proper preparation.

All the great religions maintain that a man is meant to live his whole life in communication with the Divine. His occasional spiritual ecstasy is but the spur to drive him ever further and deeper in his discipleship. In all, there are given certain seemingly pedestrian exercises which, if persisted in, will from time to time unveil the glory of God. For the Christian these are, basically, prayer, the use of the sacraments and Bible reading. They are the acts a Christian performs which to his unbelieving neighbour are just so many meaningless and time-consuming habits. And yet to the Christian himself these are his spiritual obligations as they have been of his worshipping parents over the last two thousand years.

He would be a strangely insensitive man who did not acknowledge the vast difficulties to-day involved in the whole idea of prayer. We find it impossible to act like our forefathers living in a pre-scientific age. We find it hard to believe that our prayers will have much influence on the weather, or that our children will be spared suffering because we have prayed regularly for them. The Book of Job, going back hundreds of years before Christ, put paid to such a simple casting of spiritual accounts. Job's drama has to do with a man who was known to be good and whose prosperity, it was thought, was the direct outcome of his virtues. Then, suddenly and unexpectedly, tragedy strikes. His prosperity turns to ruin, his children are killed by a series of catastrophes, and he himself loses his health in a wasting sickness.

Conscious of his own rectitude, Job thinks he has a right to rail against God and to accuse Him for His falsity in not taking care of His most faithful servant. True, in the story as we have it in our Bibles, we are given an unreal though a happy ending. But we all have met Job—more than once most of us—and we have been shocked by the inexplicable 'bad luck' that has dogged his life. Some of us, without any conceit or self-pity, may feel at heart that there is something of Job even in us. We have prayed, and prayed; but apparently God has not heard our prayers, certainly not in the way we were brought up to believe. And what is true of ourselves is even more true of the world of chaos and disunity for which we intercede every day. And so we begin to wonder whether we have not outgrown prayer and whether we should not look elsewhere.

But if the false idea that the object of prayer is to change God's mind and His good will towards us is now properly and wholly discredited, this does not mean that prayer is a habit of childhood which we have outgrown.

There are two convictions about prayer which remain stable and unmoved through the centuries. There is the grace of God who has given His human creation the ability to pray and thus to enter into communication and fellowship with Himself. Added to this is the fact that God has invested humanity with such dignity so as to limit the

exercise of His own power without man's effective co-
operation in prayer. We are certain that God's purposes of
love will not be finally frustrated, and that therefore in the
end God will have His way; nevertheless it is the Christian
belief that as the doing of His will can be accelerated
through the prayers of the faithful, so it can be slowed
down if they fail to pray.

Should any bright young sceptic wish to laugh this conviction out of court, most of us would be able to answer
that we have been privileged to know men of prayer and,
apart altogether from the influence of prayer on a third
party—animate or inanimate—there is no doubt about its
effect on the praying man himself. Meeting someone who
is patently a man of God is a humbling experience, and a
holy one. We know we have been in touch with the sacred.

Yet the difficulties remain. What are we to do about our
prayers? Let me recommend a very valuable paperback
which was first published in the United States in 1965, and
in this country last year. It is by the Reverend Malcolm
Boyd, who has made himself well known as an heroic witness to 'way out' causes over the last twelve years. His
simple little book has as its title *Are You Running With Me,
Jesus?* [1] and consists of a collection of his own prayers and
short meditations. In the Introduction he writes: 'I have
come to learn that real prayer is not so much talking to
God as just sharing his presence. . . . I am able to live in a
kind of Christian nonchalance rooted in a trust of God
which severs the old double-standard morality game I used
to play with him. I can no longer conceive of lying to him
in proper Old English or any other style of speech. I feel
free to be completely myself with him. In a given situation
where I know he is with me (perhaps in another person, or
persons), I speak out of that deep trust and love which can

[1] S.C.M. Press, 6/-.

spring only from a healthy, tried, and authentic freedom.
. . . Prayer, I have learned, is more my response to God
than a matter of my own initiative. I believe Jesus Christ
prays *in* me as well as *for* me. But my response is sporadic,
moody, now despairing, now joyful, corrupted by my self-
love and desire to manipulate Christ's love. The community of Christ incarnates prayer in its essential life, and
my own prayer is a part of this.'

And later in the same Introduction, Malcolm Boyd
answers the question which he knows many will ask: 'It
has been asked by some persons why this book is not entitled, *Am I Running With You, Jesus?* The query over-
looks the fact that my prayer life, as the state of my
spirituality, is neither very respectable nor quite correct.
Needless to say, I am a self-centred man, sinfully immersed
in my own welfare and concerns, attempting to manipulate
God, and often lost in my own self-love and self-pity. . . .
I have not tried to root out the person of Malcolm Boyd
from these prayers, for it was Malcolm Boyd who prayed
them. Prayer must be personal, imbedded in the ground of
one's own being as a person meeting God.'

In writing such as this, one who has demonstrated
beyond all argument that his faith must be lived out in the
besetting problems of the world shows that there is no con-
flict between the sacred and the secular.

VI. THE LIFE OF FAITH (2)

CHRISTIANS have often failed to play their part in everyday life, not just personally and domestically, but in all that makes up human society. This is to be deplored, but the opposite is equally unsatisfactory. History denies that the Christians who have accomplished most in social reform and human advance have been too involved to leave any time for prayer and worship. On the contrary; the evidence goes to show that the Christians who have been the pioneers in working for the realization of the Kingdom of God have been men and women who recognized the importance of the means of Grace, and have been punctilious in their employment.

Often reformers have been reformers only because they prayed. Had they failed to pray they might well have failed to secure the reformation they worked for—indeed they might not have even been aware of the work waiting to be done. A Christian who is so embroiled in all the ordinary things of daily life is in danger of forgetting the existence of the sacred, and the impact the sacred reality ought to be making on all that constitutes human existence.

As has already been said, we cannot tie God down to the moments when He will choose to reveal Himself to us. There is a continuing sense of the mystery of God which is lost if we begin to think of Him rather as Object than as Subject. And there must be, because of our human limitations, something incomprehensible and unknown about the God we worship or He ceases to be more than the agency whereby we work magic on our own behalf. In spite of the fullness of revelation in Jesus Christ, God Almighty remains the God who hideth Himself; and if God is to be God we would not have it otherwise.

All those who have grown into being masters of the

spiritual life have left this unpredictability on record. The well-known occurrence in all religious development is so general that 'the dark night of the soul' when a man is despairingly aware of the absence of God, is seen to be common to all. For all the earth-bound nature of our own experiences, we know that we can neither account for nor guarantee those revelations of the Divine Splendour which at some time or other have come to us. Suddenly we say with deceitful Jacob: 'How awesome is this place: this is none other than the House of God, and this is the Gate of Heaven'. Such knowledge does not depend on any spiritual qualities of our own; it is as if God is determined to make it clear to mankind that His good tidings of salvation are not a consequence of any human virtues. Always His redemption is the result of His own initiative. Never is it the result of our own activities, however disinterested or useful —'not of works, lest any man should boast'. The *mysterium tremendum* cannot be organized or made to fit in with our preconceived requirements.

Nevertheless, Christian history has evolved a regular pattern of worship—of a man's getting in touch with his God. And the practice that is uniquely Christian is the Holy Communion. Other religions pray; other religions have their sacred scriptures; other religions develop a closely-knit fellowship among fellow-devotees. But to-day, whatever the influence of Mithraism and other mystery religions on the early Church, Christianity alone exalts the sacred meal into the most powerful expression of God's power and His love. Although we cannot order God to come down any staircase of our choosing, we seek to use the means of Grace which we believe He through His Holy Spirit has given us. It is our conviction that our duty is to keep any appointment God decides to make, and we are convinced that He honours our obedience whether we are aware of the Divine

Presence or not. After all our apprehension of God's presence is basically of no importance. We do not go to meet with Him for what we can get out of it but because we are trying to do His will as we understand it. Whether He makes His presence known to us is His decision and not ours.

We are unable to question the fact that there is something different about the man who makes time for his prayers from the man so occupied with the affairs of this world—often good and worthy causes, let me add—that he finds no time to pray. It is not even true that those who do not pray get more done than those who do. Apart from anything else, there is through prayer the release of an integrating force, which helps to iron out a man's compulsions and neuroses and results in a far more efficient and smoothly-working time-table.

For many Christians the time they hold themselves most effectively before God is the Service of Holy Communion. Above all else, it symbolizes the sanctification of daily life. And this it does by taking simple foods like bread and wine, and using them to convey the reality and life-giving power of Christ's Body and Blood. We are always tempted to separate what Studdert-Kennedy used to call the bread of the altar from the bread of the street. But there is fundamentally no difference between the sacred and the secular, for all life is God's and He has set His seal on the whole of life. Nothing helps us more thoroughly to realize the truth of this than the Holy Communion.

Moreover, it is the one service which is never exhausted by familiarity. Its essential mystery for ever escapes us, and we recognize that there is always far more to learn and far more to assimilate. Every time we partake of the Sacrament, we are made aware of its sacred wonder and we never penetrate further than the outer court of its grandeur.

Small wonder that St. Francis de Sales wrote in his *Introduction to the Devout Life*:

> If men of the world ask you why you communicate so often, tell them that it is that you may learn to love God; that you may be cleansed from imperfections, set free from trouble, comforted in affliction, strengthened in weakness. Tell them that there are two manner of men that need frequent Communion: those who are perfect since, being ready, they were much to blame did they not come to the Source and Fountain of all perfection; and the imperfect, that they may learn how to become perfect: the strong lest they become weak, and the weak that they may become strong; the sick that they may be healed, and the sound lest they sicken. Tell them that you, weak and imperfect and ailing, need frequently to communicate with your Perfection, your Strength, your Physician. Tell them that those who are but little engaged in worldly affairs should communicate often, because they have leisure; and those who are heavily pressed with business, because they stand so much in need of help; and that he who is hardworked needs frequent and substantial food. Tell them that you receive the Blessed Sacrament that you may learn to receive It better. One rarely does well what one seldom does.

Its inexpressible value has been experienced by thousands upon thousands of Christians in generation after generation. It has heartened them in their daily lives, in all the crises that humanity has to endure, and it has comforted and lightened their dying beds, enabling them to face the last river bravely as they approach it fortified by the Body and Blood of Christ.

For innumerable simple people, as well as for many of the learned, it has signified the invasion of this world by the Eternal, by the Holy. These are not for the most part men and women living as monks and nuns in cloistered seclusion; these are Christians who are fully engaged in all that makes up the secular world, but who nevertheless experience the reality of the Sacred in the Sacrament with the result that more and more the sacred penetrates the secular.

One would not expect its efficacy to be measurable by scientific means. Yet there is convincing truth in words attributed to our Lord: 'by their fruits ye shall know them'; of which truth the humble, devout and faithful communicant is a shining example.

In these days, believers generally are sadly aware of the unhappy divisions in the Church of Christ. Most of them accept it as their duty to do all they can to help to heal the wounds in Christ's mystical Body; but never are they more conscious of the scandal of a divided Christendom than when they take part in a Communion service, whether it be called the Lord's Supper, the Mass, the Eucharist or what you will. Whatever else the growing together of Christians over the last years has done, it has certainly restored the Holy Communion to its central position in corporate worship. And its own sacredness has given great impetus to the movement for unity. It is part of its nature to expose the sinfulness of the churches as they tolerate their disunity without an overwhelming sense of guilt and shame. In the Upper Room at the time when our Lord was instituting the Sacrament He prayed that all who believed in Him might be one, and the lamentable and dangerous history of a fragmented world is in tragic measure due to the painful history of the fragmentation of the Church of God.

> No barrier of race or creed or nation
> Can break that sacramental comradeship of
> bread and wine
> As long as mankind prays,
> 'Our Father who art in heaven.'

So wrote an anonymous writer, and his words speak to our condition to-day.

For many the Holy Communion makes the fact of Calvary present to the worshipper. The central mystery of the Christian faith is the death and resurrection of Jesus Christ. We talk about the atonement and explanations galore have been offered over the years. None of them stand up very well, and we are left with a bald statement which all believers would accept that on the Cross Jesus effected something without which mankind could not be saved. We understand the biblical comparison between the fact of our Lord's death and the deliverance of the children of Israel from their bondage in Egypt. And we believe that what was accomplished in the physical realm in the release from slavery is somehow accomplished in man's total being —though we do not thoroughly know why—by our Lord's death and His being raised to life again.

Sometimes the event of Calvary may have been sentimentalized; sometimes it may have been exaggerated at the expense of the rest of Jesus' incarnate life; sometimes it may have been cheapened by its crude and over-dramatic presentation. But there is absolutely no doubt that the process of 'coming to the Cross'—however difficult this may be to explain in theological terms—has transformed the lives of myriads of people. The Cross is from all evidence the supreme place of the divine-human encounter; and from the beginning of the Christian era it has remained both the means and the symbol of man's salvation.

There must be very few people who are not acquainted with men and women whose lives have been completely transformed as a result. But its potency has to be recognized as beyond human explanation or analysis. It is without doubt the breaking in of the Eternal into our world —it is the Supreme Sacred Event of man's renewal.

It needs no underlining that the effects of the Holy Communion reach out into every aspect of the human situation. The fact that Jesus chose everyday things like bread and wine helps to divinize the whole of life; and the more the Christian enters into its mystery, the more the secular has to retreat before the advance of the sacred—not now identifying the secular with the rational, but realizing that the world we live in is God's world and acting accordingly.

This conviction leaves no part of living untouched. Divine obedience becomes more and more the significant part of every decision, and even in this scientific age, a man can work and eat, and think and play, can make love and can go to sleep, all deliberately in God's presence. There is nothing magical or fantastic about this. If St. Paul is right when he says that in Christ we live and move and have our being, then our task is to make conscious that which is all the time true whether we are aware of it or not.

Generations have found the inspiration for this kind of life in the experience and writings of Brother Lawrence of the Resurrection, whose life covered nearly the whole of the seventeenth century. Having served as a soldier and, later, lived as a hermit, he entered the Carmelite monastery at Paris in 1649. It was while working in the kitchen that one day he looked outside, and an apparently dead tree spoke to him of the reality of God. For the rest of his life he taught and himself exemplified the practice of the presence of God, which, he believed, could be the fruit of the imagination or of the intellect, or of both.

It is no doubt true that in a predominantly secular age, the sacred will be squeezed out unless of set purpose we make time for it. There may be one or two, but the proportion is infinitesimally small, who are in danger of ignoring the secular and of being swamped by the sacred.

But such instances are very much the exception and not the rule. It is the argument of this book that the Christian must play his full part as a human being in the whole of life; but in general pressure of this normal living is so strong that there is little likelihood of its being undervalued. The peril is all the other way: this life of space and time so demands our attention that, if we are not careful, we shall put all our eggs into this world's basket and forget altogether that there is another world than this. Hence the urgent need to make full use of all possible means to foster the reality of the Eternal in all that constitutes our lives.

When our Lord told His disciples that they were *in* the world but not *of* the world, He was not asking them to withdraw from ordinary workaday life; He was, however, urging them to recollect continually that they were more than other animals in that they had been given the power to communicate with God and were destined for God. Never should they forget the sacred in their legitimate concern for the secular. Thus it was, that our Lord prayed those well-known words: 'I pray not that thou shouldest take them out of the world but that thou shouldest keep them from the evil . . . .'

The life of faith calls us to live as the sons of God who, in Christ, we already are.

VII. THE WAY FORWARD

I HAVE just been watching an interview with Pier Paolo
Pasolini on television. He is the director of the film 'The
Gospel According to Matthew', which has received rave
notices both in this country and in America. It is in no
way like the more usual biblical epics from Hollywood,
which generally turn out to be massive spectaculars with
plenty of sex, violence and bloodshed. True, there is
violence in Pasolini's film, but it is the violence of words,
the violence of character which is displayed. And coming
back to a reading of St. Matthew after seeing the film, one
is struck by its violence, lending little colour to the sentimentalized picture of the 'gentle Jesus, meek and mild' to
which people cling long after their childhood.

But cinema goers have been interested in the film, not
only for its quality but because it has been directed by one
who is an avowed Communist, and indeed whose last pro-
duction was condemned as blasphemous.

During the fascinating TV interview, Pasolini left us in
no doubt that he believed that the world itself was sacred
—not just Jesus, a more than human figure—but the fields
themselves, the whole of life. He was passionately eager to
recapture the sacred; and in his film he hoped that those
who saw it would be helped to look at their own lives, at
the whole of existence in a new way. To him, life is more
than eating, sleeping, working and copulating: it is more
than the sum total of physical experiences, or even of intellectual exercises—in fact it embraces far more than we
normally realize. This widening of our horizons emotion-
ally, which he does for us by enlarging and intensifying
them visually, is an unveiling of the sacredness of the world.
Pasolini is probably not yet ready to call it God's world,

but the vision he gives us is the opening of the eyes we all need.

St. Frances de Sales used to say that as you learn to walk by walking and to swim by swimming, so you learn to love by loving. In a world which is increasingly evacuated of the divine, we can stay the progress—or perhaps better, regress—by making time for God, by recognizing that we are part of His creation, and that the whole world falls within the orbit of His redemptive activity.

How this will affect men and women differs from person to person. The famous Albert Schweitzer expressed it in his own practical philosophy, that of reverence for life. If we are humble and willing to learn, we shall all find our own way.

Again, let it be stated that this book does not contest the proper secularization of life. But secularization does not call for abdication on God's part. True faith is to use the means which God puts at our disposal. The increasing skill of a surgeon, or the discoveries of an atomic physicist do not send God packing. They do not require that men should live without reference to God. They ask for something far more difficult, namely, that in a world where a vast majority of our generation can get on perfectly well without God, those who are Christians make time and opportunity to find the reality of God behind, what others would call, natural phenomena.

What it comes to is this: we do not embrace religion for what we can get out of it; we no longer go to God with a lengthy grocery list; we have ceased to run a profit and loss account with Him. But we refuse to believe that God has deserted His world. Rather we are convinced that man reaches his true destiny only when he tries to live in conscious fellowship with God. Not exclusively, because the fellowship goes on even in man's unconscious moments. But the first essential is that man should be awakened to an awareness of God, an awareness which has to be cultivated and deepened by all legitimate means open to him.

One of the most obvious faults of the western world is its arrogance. Over the centuries it has grown increasingly self-sufficient, and in doing so it has tended to diminish the cultures and civilizations of other peoples. Because the west falls more easily into a materialistic way of life, it is constantly tempted to assert that its way is the highest way, the best way, and unless on his guard the man of the west finds himself talking patronizingly of 'lesser breeds without the law'.

No one has any desire to diminish the wonderful things that occidental man has accomplished, but he is pathetically stupid if he regards his own achievements as being the valid criterion for the whole world.

I can, for example, remember well going to Burma just before beginning my time in South Africa, and talking with a professor of the University at Rangoon who was astonished beyond understanding by the *apartheid* policies of South Africa with its conception of white superiority and the inferiority of other races. 'How can they act like this?', he asked me. 'At the most their civilization goes back 2,000 years; ours goes back 6,000 years.'

Not alone in racial terms, but in a variety of spheres the white man is confident that he has progressed further than other races. And with reason. He is undoubtedly first in the scientific field, but his success has not been limited to the world's betterment. No other peoples have been so successful in inventing—and using—weapons of destruction. The account does not show only gain.

Of all the animals, none is so predatory as man; and of all men, none is so predatory as the white man. One has only to read a book like Alan Moorehead's *The Fatal*

Impact, which tells the story of the opening up of the Pacific by men from Europe, to learn again to one's horror their influence for evil upon both the human and the animal population. As we read with shame what happened to the Tahitians of that famous island and the Aboriginals of Australia, we recognize what David Livingstone failed to recognize, that the coming of the Gospel (alas, too often a sectarian and totally inadequate faith) plus the opening up of the country to commerce and to some European national flag have by no means always spelt prosperity and contentment.

Now that with the rapidity of transport the size of the globe has been hugely diminished, Western pride is not as self-confident as it used to be. At long last the west is beginning to realize that it has much to learn as well as much to give.

In particular this comes as the Western Christian for the first time meets the believers of other faiths. He may well discover to his surprise that the other faiths have retained a belief in the sacred which he himself has had to discard. The practice of prayer and meditation in some of the oriental religions brings him into a new world where the divine is everywhere present and has neither to be explained away nor apologized for. He finds an attitude which is in complete contrast to the activism of the west, and a people to whom their faith is of paramount importance.

There was a time when missionaries tried to justify their own ways by condemning all others as so many heathen practices. But such an attempt could be made only in direct opposition to the teaching of Holy Scripture. For example, we read in the Acts of the Apostles (10 : 34, 35) that 'God is not a respecter of persons, but in every nation he who fears him and does what is right is acceptable to him'.

And it is to be hoped that we realize better than our

fathers that in going to strange countries there to proclaim
the Gospel, we do not take Christ to a place where He has
never been, we go, by God's grace, to unveil the Christ who
is already there and who has been there all the time. Again
we read : 'He that comes to God must believe that he exists
and that he rewards those who try to find him' (Hebrews
11 : 6).

The way forward therefore is not to resist the proper
secularization of life, above all not by any ecclesiastical
institution or religious machine. Rather it is to counter-
attack, to make bold to claim that every seeker after truth,
be he scientist, artist or *guru*, is both acknowledged and
honoured by Him who said : 'I am the Truth'. The battle-
front does not lie here. The battle-front is to be found
wherever men deny the Divine Presence, or where men live
as though God does not exist and who in consequence order
their lives without any reference to Him.

How better can we define the heart of the Christian faith
and the reality of the Sacred than those words which come
in the first epistle of St. John : 'Behold, what manner of
love the Father hath bestowed upon us that we should be
called sons of God' (1 John 3 : 1). Then in the translation
of the Jerusalem Bible the author writes :

> My dear people, we are already the children of God,
> but what we are to be in the future has not yet been
> revealed ;
> all we know is, that when it is revealed
> we shall be like him
> because we shall see him as he really is.

Nothing can alter the fact that this is God's world.
Because it is God's world it is holy, and therefore the Sacred
and not the Secular will have the last word.